Original title:
A Scarf's Quiet Tale

Copyright © 2025 Creative Arts Management OÜ
All rights reserved.

Author: Vivienne Beaumont
ISBN HARDBACK: 978-1-80586-152-2
ISBN PAPERBACK: 978-1-80586-624-4

Unraveling Moments

In winter's chill, a vibrant twist,
A tangled tale that can't be missed.
It danced with wind, it flapped like wings,
Oh, the joy that this fabric brings!

Knotted loops and frayed ends play,
It likes to wander, drift away.
Caught in a door, a playful snare,
Chasing squirrels, oh, what a scare!

Colors bright and patterns bold,
A treasure of warmth, a story told.
Yet no one knows the secrets spun,
In each little stitch, there's so much fun!

And at the party, it steals the scene,
With unexpected moves, it acts so keen.
Onholders toast with laughter's cheer,
Telling tales of wild frontier!

The Whispering Weave

Once it sat on a shelf so grand,
Proudly boasting, it started to stand.
But with one sneeze, it slipped and fell,
Whispering secrets, oh, what a spell!

It bounces 'round in the laundry's whirl,
Caught on a sock, oh, what a twirl!
Absent-mindedly worn on a cat,
A fuzzy crown, imagine that!

Each thread a joke, each weave a pun,
It twirls 'round tables, oh, what fun!
Accident-prone, it leads a life,
Of hiccups and giggles, never strife!

At dusk it dreams, of days gone by,
Under the stars in the evening sky.
For though it's worn, its spirits high,
A wise old fabric, always sly!

Threads of Whispered Memories

In the corner, a twirl of old thread,
Holding secrets that once were said.
It tickles the nose, a soft little tease,
As laughter escapes with the slightest breeze.

Worn by the cat, a colorful mess,
Meowing tales of warmth and finesse.
Each stitch a giggle, each knot a cheer,
Knitted stories that bring back the year.

The Weave of Yesterday's Warmth

A jumble of colors, a fabric parade,
Whispering tales of the fun that we made.
In forgotten drawers, it puffs with delight,
Stitching together both daydreams and night.

Longing for hugs in the cold winter air,
It hops off the shelf like it's ready to share.
With a pat and a flip, it dances with glee,
It's the life of the party, just wait and see!

Embracing Chill in Soft Hues

A chill in the air, but it giggles with glee,
Wrap me up closely, I'm just what you need.
Soft hues like candy, a playful embrace,
Warming you up in this chilly space.

Frosty adventures, it pulls you along,
With whimsical threads, it hums a sweet song.
Each flair and each twist, a comic refrain,
Who knew that the cold could vibe with such gain?

The Fabric of Forgotten Journeys

In a suitcase, it naps, dreaming of roads,
Of sunsets and laughter, of whimsical codes.
It whispers of places where mischief was born,
And tells of mishaps on each woven yarn.

Tugged through the crowds, a sly little slip,
Taking wild rides on the world's crazy trip.
With each little tear, a new story's begun,
A fabric of journeys where laughter's the fun.

The Woven Heartbeat

In a drawer where dust does play,
A yarn with stories tucked away.
It twirled and spun with such delight,
A dance of fibers, taking flight.

With every twist, a giggle's spark,
It whispered secrets, loud and stark.
A purple patch, a greenish hue,
It dreams of odd-shaped socks for two.

Echoes of the Weave

In the corner, an old loom sighs,
Woven laughter fills the skies.
With each pull of thread, a quirk appears,
And every pattern, it draws in cheers.

A ragged edge, a loopy turn,
For comical twirls, our passions burn.
It's not just fabric, but tales galore,
With puns and jokes, who could ask for more?

Taking Flight with Wool

Oh the yarn, it dreams of flight,
With every stitch, it takes a bite.
A little bird perched on my head,
Laughing at the fashion it led.

With pom-poms plumped and tassels free,
It flutters like a cheeky bee.
In every loop, a comedy grows,
As I trip over toes, goodness knows!

Whispers of the Threads

Threads tangled up, oh what a sight,
Gossiping softly, all through the night.
They plot and scheme with every nudge,
In hitches and knots, they just won't budge.

In laughter, they weave their daily tale,
Of crafty colors, bright as a gale.
So next time you see a piece so grand,
Know it spun from mischief, as planned!

Ties of Tenderness

In a drawer, a twist of fluff,
Once stylish, but just a bit tough.
Worn with pride in a fancy race,
Now just a ghost of a twirl and grace.

Draped on a lamp, it sways with glee,
As the cat pounces—then laughs at me.
Whispers of warmth, a neck's best friend,
In the breeze, it says, 'Let's not pretend.'

Wrapped in Memories

A pop of color in the closet's maze,
Recalling times of wild, silly days.
Around my neck, quite the bold affair,
Like a comedian, it's always there.

With every knot, a memory tied,
Of clumsy dances and awkward pride.
It's seen my laughs and heard my sighs,
As it sways in laughter, it never lies.

Threads of a Past Dream

Each thread a story, a giggle, a wink,
Tangled in tales, oh, what do you think?
From grandma's chest, to my working chair,
It's a comical route we've traveled to share.

In a twist, it turns to an artful mess,
Dare I say it, what a bold dress!
Stitched with dreams that dance in the night,
A tapestry of fun, a joyous sight.

Tones of Gentle Hues

Draped on the shoulders of laughter and fun,
It's a jester's cap in a world on the run.
Each color a giggle, each fabric a cheer,
Whisking away any hint of a tear.

In the closet it giggles, snickers in stash,
Colorful chaos transforming in a flash.
It keeps the secrets of joys yet to bloom,
In a corner's delight, it banishes gloom.

Lace and Lament

Once I wore this lace with glee,
It danced in winds so wild and free.
Then came the day, oh what a sight,
It snagged on bushes, took flight!

A tale of threads that did betray,
While I was lost in dreams of play.
It tangled with the dog named Lou,
And now it's just a chew toy too!

Each knot a laugh, each rip a grin,
A saga born from sheer chagrin.
Oh what a mess, what jolly plight,
My lacey woes turned sheer delight!

Wind's Embrace

The wind once hugged me oh so tight,
It loved my scarf, a charming sight.
But in a gust, it snatched away,
My scarf took off, I yelled, "Hey, hey!"

Like a kite gone rogue, it soared so far,
I chased it down, a hopeful star.
Through puddles deep and bushes wide,
That wily scarf, my pride, it died!

It danced with leaves and teased the bees,
And made the squirrels bow their knees.
So here I stand, my antics bold,
A story shared, for laughs retold!

Tales Knitted in Time

In grandma's hands, the yarn did twirl,
With stitches tight, she made it swirl.
But every loop had tales to tell,
Of mishaps, laughter—oh so swell!

A tangle here, a knot there too,
Each faux pas, a story grew.
With every stitch and every purl,
A crazy adventure gave way to whirl!

Once, it slipped from her woolly lap,
And danced away—oh what a flap!
The dog wore it like a fancy hat,
We laughed so hard, we fell—splat!

Textures of the Heart

With fluffy bits and colors bright,
My cozy wrap brought pure delight.
But one fateful day, it slipped my tie,
And flew away, oh me, oh my!

A comedy in every thread,
As I chased it down, filled with dread.
Through puddles and mud, it made its stand,
That rascal wrap, oh how it planned!

Now stories swirl around the block,
Of my mad dash and silly shock.
Friends all tease, but I just smile,
For every laugh's worth every mile!

Woven Joys

In colors bright, it wraps around,
A tale of laughter, woven sound.
It fought the breeze on a windy day,
With every twist, it danced away.

A cat took hold, it chased with glee,
It tangled up, oh, what a spree!
With every knot, a funny sight,
It bounced and flopped, a pure delight.

Touches of the Past

Once dropped on the floor amidst the mess,
Memories linger, I must confess.
A childhood game, a tug-of-war,
Brought giggles loud, who could ask for more?

Its threads hold whispers of days gone by,
A time when socks were worn awry.
Stitched with care, yet full of quirks,
It knew our laughs, those silly perks.

Hidden Warmth

Snuggled tight, it kept me warm,
Through frosty nights, it did perform.
Yet when it slipped, oh, what a tease,
Wrapped 'round a chair, with so much ease!

A partner in crime for many a trick,
Pulled from a drawer—it makes me tick.
It waves 'hello' in a playful dance,
Breathes life into every chance.

Sentiments in the Stitch

Each stitch a giggle, each loop a grin,
Crafting tales where fun begins.
Tangled threads, oh, what a sight,
Wrapped in joy, it feels so right!

A quirky gift from Auntie May,
With patterns that lead the eye astray.
It whispers secrets of laughter shared,
In every fiber, love declared.

Coats of Whimsy

In the closet, bright colors clash,
A purple coat with a green mustache.
Hats that giggle and mittens that dance,
In this fashion show, there's no second chance.

Buttons play tag and zippers zoom,
Pants that tumble, creating a room.
Slippers that wiggle, socks that joke,
Each piece of clothing, a whimsical poke.

Scarves that whisper secrets of flair,
Twirls and swirls, they do not care.
All dressed up for a silly parade,
In this wardrobe, laughter is made.

Every coat has its own little tale,
Of snowball fights and a dog's happy wail.
In the corner, an old shoe grins wide,
With fashion so fun, we can't help but pride.

A Whispered Journey

In the chilly breeze, a story unfurls,
A knit cap is teased by curls and swirls.
The puffer jacket gives a teasing spin,
While the wind whispers tales, let the fun begin.

A travel bag rolling with old stickers,
It hums a tune that always flickers.
A pair of gloves that spark a keen laugh,
Who knew a trip could start with a gaff?

The boots stumble, they trip over stones,
While the jacket groans, it's feeling like bones.
In this journey of fabric and thread,
Every stitch has a giggle to spread.

By the end, oh the tales that will soar,
Knitwear whispers secrets galore.
From the cobbled streets to heights we'll roam,
With laughter, we'll always find our way home.

Strands of Solace

In the corner, a lonely shoelace sighs,
As socks pair up, under bright sunny skies.
One thread jests about tangled-up fate,
While the others just giggle and contemplate.

Fuzzy sweaters cuddle, knitting their plot,
While the hoodie is busy—giving it a shot.
The headband rolls eyes, it's seen all before,
In fabric's embrace, laughter's never a bore.

A scarf lays low, a quiet onlooker,
As the bright hues of night start to hook her.
Beneath twinkling lights, they chase dreams anew,
In this fabric fest, there's joy in the crew.

Every string ties us, no one left behind,
In a cozy little corner, the silly unwind.
Soft laughter mingles in each cozy fold,
In strands of comfort, more warmth to be told.

The Threads We Keep

In the attic, a relic of wear and tear,
An old parka sits, with stories to share.
His zippers, once fast, now have a slow creak,
But every patch has a memory to speak.

A quilt of colors, soft as a dream,
Each piece stitched tight with a humorous theme.
The pockets hold candies from long ago fun,
In the world of textiles, our laughter's not done.

Ties from dances, and caps from the sun,
All woven together, a tapestry run.
With threads that connect us, so vibrant and neat,
In the fabric of life, funny stories repeat.

As we gather around, tales intertwine,
The moments we cherish, always align.
From fibers of friendship to laughter-filled leaps,
These are the treasures—oh, the threads we keep.

Wrapped in the Breath of Winter

Wrapped snugly in layers, so bright,
Flapping around, what a sight!
Snowflakes giggle, they dance with glee,
Laughing at whispers, oh let's be free!

I twirl and I swirl, a cotton parade,
While friends take turns, in laughter they wade.
With every unfurl, and a twist of the thread,
I'm the life of the party, like it or dread!

The chill in the air joins the playful tune,
I keep them all warm, from morning till noon.
Frosty noses peeking with mischief galore,
Together we chuckle, oh, who could ask for more?

So here's to the giggles in winter's embrace,
A bundle of joy in this frosty race.
With colors so vibrant, it's hard not to grin,
Wrapped in this warmth, let the fun times begin!

The Veil of Gentle Moonglow

In shadows, I shimmer, a glimmering guise,
Draped over shoulders, a treasure that flies.
Whispers at midnight, stories unfold,
Of dreams and of chuckles in fabrics so bold.

Oh how I twinkle beneath skies so bright,
A comedic companion, whilst lost in the night.
With each gentle breeze, I play peek-a-boo,
Tickling your cheeks like the first dance in dew.

I catch all the secrets of laughter and sighs,
Gamers and jesters hold me with pride.
In starlit embrace, let the jests take their flight,
My fibers remember each giggle, each bite.

As dawn starts to blush, the shenanigans fade,
In morning's bright light, new mischief is laid.
But hush now, my friend, don't forget our fun,
With warmth in your heart, the laughter's not done!

Stitches of Solitude

Alone with my thoughts, I weave a fine thread,
Knitting up giggles where others once fled.
The clack of my needles, a rhythmic delight,
Creating pure joy in the stillness of night.

Each loop a memory, a peek and a pry,
Of moments spent laughing, just you and I.
Oh, solitude's laughter, a quirky affair,
With ramblings and chuckles that float through the air.

I craft little hats for the mice in my room,
Who wear them with pride, and dance to the bloom.
Together we frolic, a quirky brigade,
In stitches of solitude, our fun can't evade.

So come closer, dear friend, enjoy the delight,
In solitude's chambers, we frolic till light.
With colors and humor, we banish the gloom,
Laugh out loud, for there's always more room!

Cozy Murmurs in the Frost

In the chill of the night, a whisper goes round,
I bob and I weave, making not a sound.
Under the moonlight, I swish and I swoosh,
Turning dull moments to a jovial push.

A fire is crackling, friends gather near,
With cozy companions, the laughter is clear.
We sip on hot cocoa, and playful remarks,
Sharing our secrets beneath twinkling sparks.

I flutter and fumble, in blankets we nest,
Each stitch a soft way to feel our best.
With every warm chuckle, my colors ignite,
In the frosty night air, we're a merry sight.

So come wrap me 'round and let laughter convene,
As cozy murmurs keep the frosty nights keen.
Together we chuckle till the break of the dawn,
In warmth and in joy, we keep carrying on!

Echoes in Every Loop

In the closet, tucked away,
A vibrant twist of yarns at play.
It whispers secrets, slightly frayed,
Of chilly nights and warmth displayed.

With each coil and every twist,
A giggle found, it can't be missed.
On windy days, it takes a flight,
An unexpected fashion plight.

In silly knots, it holds the tales,
Of frozen fingers and daring sails.
It dances 'round the coffee spill,
A trusted friend through every thrill.

So when you wear it, don't forget,
The laughter shared, and silly bets.
A tangled mess, yet somehow neat,
This woven joy, a comfy seat.

Revisiting Threads

Once I found a thread so bright,
It sparkled in the morning light.
I pulled it gently, oh what fun,
  Out came tales of anyone!

It wrapped my neck, then slipped away,
  To join a cat in wild play.
With every twist and cheerful tug,
Brought forth a giggle, warm and snug.

Tall tales of wine and party hats,
A dance with dogs, and even cats.
It tangled up in laughter's embrace,
  A fabric tale, it found its place.

So when it whispers sweet and low,
Remember all the things we know.
For every knot and funky spin,
Is laughter stitched right from within.

Patterns of the Heart

In colors bold and patterns wild,
A fabric born, once soft and mild.
It wraps around with silly grace,
A hug from friends, a warm embrace.

Each loop and twist a tale to share,
Of mischief found in frosty air.
It caught the breeze, then took a dive,
Where laughter flowed and dreams revived.

When chilly winds began to howl,
It sheltered thoughts and goofy growls.
A canvas of our joyful quests,
In every fold, a friend suggests.

So as you wear this cheerful thread,
Recall the jokes and all we said.
For in each stitch, a love so deft,
A testament of joy that's left.

The Fabric of Friendship

A colorful weave of joy and cheer,
A gentle tug, come lend an ear.
It holds our stories, bold and bright,
And wraps us snug on winter nights.

From coffee spills to playful pranks,
It catches moments, loves, and flanks.
A twirl of laughter in every fold,
A treasure kept, worth more than gold.

Sometimes it slips, oh what a mess,
Yet brings us pause and sweet distress.
In every pull, a memory's thread,
Of silly times that gently spread.

So gather round, let's share a laugh,
In woven bonds, we find our path.
For in this fabric, quirks and all,
Are friendships true, that will not fall.

The Comfort of Old Threads

In a drawer, tucked away,
Lies a relic, soft and gray.
With a frayed edge and a stain,
It whispers secrets of the mundane.

Once it donned a dapper flair,
Now it's lost its warm repair.
Yet wrapped around a sneezy head,
It's a crown fit for a comfy bed.

The dog thinks it's a cozy toy,
Tugging fiercely, oh what joy!
But it remains a trusty friend,
A laughter-filled, threadbare blend.

With each loop, a memory spins,
Of wild days and silly wins.
Though it's worn and old, it's true,
It's the best thing to wrap around you.

Cascades of Comfort

Once a vibrant shade of red,
Now it drapes like a sleepy bed.
It twirls and swirls in funny poses,
Catching crumbs and random roses.

Around my neck, it likes to dance,
With every gust, it takes a chance.
A fashion statement, or my best mate?
Despite its style, it's a twist of fate.

In wind, it flaps like a great big bird,
Clinging tight, it's often heard.
As laughter spills with every knot,
It makes me feel like quite the hotshot.

So here it stays, with its tales and glee,
A tangled mess, a sight to see.
In all its chaos, warmth unfolds,
A funny story in fabric it holds.

Shades of Comfort

Worn edges blend with faded hues,
It wraps me up, the perfect ruse.
In shades of coffee, navy, and cream,
It feels like snuggling in a dream.

Oh! What secrets does it keep?
Stories of naps and laughter deep.
A wardrobe gem that's past its prime,
Spilling giggles with every rhyme.

In winter's chill, it comes alive,
A source of joy, where jokes survive.
It wraps my throat, all snug and tight,
As I dance around in pure delight.

So let it hang and let it sway,
With every twist, it finds its way.
For in its folds, I see the fun,
A silly journey never done.

The Gentle Wrap

Draped around like a cozy hug,
It draws me in with a gentle tug.
Its fabric crinkles with every twist,
A whimsical friend that can't be missed.

Gathering stories, thread by thread,
Whimsical life it's gently fed.
In a swirl of color, laughter springs,
As it tickles my neck and softly sings.

Caught in a breeze, it takes a flight,
Twirling past, what a silly sight!
With every flutter, it shows a grin,
A playful spirit wrapped within.

So here I go, with flair and cheer,
In my lively wrap, I'll persevere.
A gentle comfort, oh so bright,
In its funny dance, I take delight.

Moments Woven Tight

In a drawer all crumpled, it lies,
Whispers of laughter, a bundle of ties.
Knots from the dog who thought it a toy,
A fabric of joy, a thread of pure joy.

Lost in a wash, now a charming heap,
It dreams of adventures, oh how it weeps.
Once it swayed with a breeze, stylish and neat,
Now it dangles on a chair, a tale bittersweet.

Hitchhiked on adventures, rides through the day,
Spilled on the table, a culinary ballet.
Pasta and sauce, oh what a sight,
But still it smiles, stitched moments tight.

In the end, it's the stories that count,
In each awkward twist, memories mount.
So here's to the fabric, worn but not shy,
It wraps up our laughter, as time flits by.

Rounded Edges of Time

Frayed at the ends, but full of delight,
It tells of the days, both fluffy and bright.
Wrapped around shoulders, a chuckle or two,
A cape for the clumsy, still sticking like glue.

Worn in the autumn, draped over the leaves,
Gathering tales that the heart believes.
From squirrel encounters to splashes in rain,
The edges are round, not a moment in vain.

It's been a dance partner, caught in a twirl,
With a wink and a giggle, about to unfurl.
Through mishaps and giggles, it holds all the charm,
A snug little hug, quite safe from all harm.

Though colors may fade and the fibers may fray,
It holds every secret and silly display.
A testament woven with laughter and cheer,
In the rounded edges, a memory here.

Soft Shadows

In the midday sun, it casts gentle twirls,
Spinning with shadows of laughter and swirls.
Caught in a breeze, it dances away,
Chasing the giggles of children at play.

Once on a chair, it sat with a sigh,
As a curious cat thought it'd learned to fly.
A pounce and a bounce, confusion ensued,
The fabric just giggled, amused and renewed.

It soaked up the spills of a party's delight,
Chocolate fingerprints from a cake gone awry.
Every stain tells a story, in soft, playful hues,
Each thread a reminder of fond rendezvous.

In the evening glow, it wraps up the night,
Holding soft shadows, basking in light.
With a wink and a nod, it gathers each tale,
Creating a quilt that will never grow stale.

The Fabric of Kindness

Stitched with affection, it drapes ever so sweet,
Hugs that are woven from our laughter fleet.
Each thread a soft whisper, kindness expressed,
A blanket of joy, in warmth we are blessed.

Dirtied by mischief, it giggles with grace,
It carries the spark of a bright, happy face.
From granddad's old pocket to bright birthday wraps,
It holds our best moments, no need for maps.

A game of hide-and-seek, it joins in the fun,
Mixing with memories, it dances and runs.
Through shared little secrets, its colors grow brighter,
Every little bump makes its spirit much lighter.

In the tapestry woven, where kindness flows free,
Each stitch tells a story, of you and of me.
So wear it with laughter, with hugs intertwined,
This fabric of warmth, forever designed.

Colors That Remember

In a drawer full of bright hues,
Lies a tale of missed cues.
Last summer's sun made it a patch,
Now it's just a comfort batch.

With polka dots and stripes in tow,
It giggles at the washing flow.
Colors clash in a funky dance,
Who knew fabric could take a chance?

When worn too often, it starts to fade,
Yet laughs at how it won't evade.
Chasing shadows, it hugs the breeze,
A fabric hero, if you please!

Oh, the stories it could tell,
From coffee spills to slips and fell.
A rainbow of memories in tangled thread,
Where laughter stitched every shred.

The Hideaway of Comfort

Crumpled in a cozy chair,
It waits with patience everywhere.
Nestled low, it hides from view,
Always ready, always true.

In moments when the chill arrives,
It leaps into action and thrives.
With each touch, it coaxes smiles,
And warmth that lasts for endless miles.

It knows the secrets of its kin,
The lost remote and where it's been.
In laughter, it finds a way to play,
Transforming dull into a bright foray.

When life gets messy, it won't pout,
Just wraps around and twists about.
A hug that words cannot convey,
Wrapped in humor, come what may.

A Tapestry of Hidden Warmth

Woven threads like a secret scheme,
It whispers softly, like a dream.
Each stitch holds a giggle, sincere,
In every fold, a grin appears.

From potluck dinners to chilly nights,
It shares its warmth, delights in lights.
Caught in a tangle, how it laughs,
Stitching stories, not just halves!

Each patch a tale, from the past it gleans,
Dances with memories, silly scenes.
A blanket of chuckles, it sways with glee,
As fabric friends sing in harmony.

It wraps the soul in playful cheer,
Banishes worries, brings good near.
Forever cherished, forever bright,
This tapestry of laughter takes flight.

Whispers Beneath the Loom

Underneath where fibers meet,
A riddle crafted, oh so neat.
Threads gossip, weaving tales,
In a fabric land where humor prevails.

Oh, the adventures, some wear and tear,
Confetti parties, just a dare!
Tickling toes with each new day,
A punchline wrapped in a cozy display.

When tangled up, it chuckles still,
At times it thinks it's part of the thrill.
Stubborn knots with a heart so grand,
Pushes back against fate's hand!

Each wrinkle, a story waiting to bloom,
A woven wonder in every room.
With a heartbeat of vibrant glee,
This great creation is wild and free.

Threads Connecting Hearts

Once wrapped around a toddler's neck,
It fluttered like a happy speck.
Through puddles, it would bravely glide,
While sipping hot cocoa side by side.

A grandparent's hug on chilly days,
In games of chase, it weaves and plays.
With every twist, a story spun,
In stitches bright, they laugh and run.

Found in a drawer, aged but bold,
Whispering secrets needing told.
In every fold, a memory found,
Adding warmth to love profound.

The Gentle Embrace of a Petal's Tale

A petal-draped shawl on a sunny morn,
Complimenting the laughter and joy reborn.
It rides the breeze, doing a little dance,
Drawing giggles from every glance.

A picnic blanket, soft and wide,
Hosting ants with nowhere to hide.
With crumbs of cake tucked in each seam,
It brings to life every silly dream.

When dogs wear it as a feathery crown,
Chasing squirrels all around the town.
It can't help but flap with a jubilant grin,
Petal soft, let the silliness begin.

Tales from the Hearth's Embrace

By the fire, so warm and bright,
A cozy tale of love takes flight.
With smores and jokes shared to the brim,
This evening is where the lights grow dim.

Grandpa's stories with laughter combined,
Whispers of yarn that two hearts bind.
From tales of adventurers bold and brash,
To socks that mysteriously clash.

Crackling flames, with a hiss and pop,
As time goes on, we never stop.
Every twist and loop, a laugh spun tight,
Wrapped in warmth, the stars shine bright.

It Speaks Without Sound

In the corner, draped across a chair,
A silent witness to joy laid bare.
Worn by all, from raucous to shy,
It giggles softly as moments fly.

A shade for games in the midday sun,
A cape for heroes, oh, what fun!
With each flip, a new plot devised,
As imagination runs wild, untamed and prized.

It holds a universe in its weaves,
Of playful schemes and make-believes.
While quiet, still, it knows the score,
With every glance, it begs for more.

Comfort Found in Every Fold

In the closet, wrapped in dreams,
Lurks a tale of yarn and seams.
Knots and tangles, oh what a sight,
Yet it warms me every night.

Worn on days, both cold and bright,
It dances with me, a funny sight.
A tumble here, a snarl up there,
I laugh out loud, beyond compare.

Once a gift from a friend so dear,
Now it's a silly game of cheer.
With every twist, a giggle slips,
As it flutters and flops like lips.

Though it's frayed and in need of rest,
It still knows how to look its best.
So here's to folds and loose embrace,
A cozy hug, my happy place.

Echoes of Cozy Journeys

Worn on trips to places grand,
A silly link to the unplanned.
It caught a breeze on rolling hills,
And wrapped around my food-filled thrills.

In a market, looking for pies,
It snagged a fruit between the thighs.
Chasing rabbits, what a sight,
Loops of laughter in morning light.

Once it hid under a picnic spread,
While squirrels plotted silly misread.
It flapped and waved, pretending to fly,
As I watched them scamper by.

Oh, the tales within each strand,
Whispered secrets from our land.
With every fold, a memory's spun,
A journey shared, a bit of fun.

Threads of Silence

In the corner, it quietly waits,
Holding tales of quirky fates.
Stitched with mischief, love, and snags,
It giggles softly between the rags.

Underneath a bed, it sighs and dreams,
Of all the laughter in moonlit beams.
Lost in the laundry, it can't complain,
Riding cycles like trains in the rain.

It once joined a dance with a bouncy cat,
A swirl of colors, and where's that mat?
It shimmied and swayed, then slipped and fell,
Pillow forts made it laugh so well.

Whispers of colors, tangled in thread,
Making jokes as it cozied in bed.
Among crayons and books, it finds its place,
A humorous hug, an old friend's grace.

Whispers in Wool

In a basket, all soft and round,
A collection of giggles, quietly found.
With every twist, a story anew,
Stitched with laughter, just for you.

As I donned it, a parade began,
My old buddy, my fuzzy plan.
We tripped through puddles, such a game,
With frolic and chaos, none felt the same.

Oh, the moments wrapped in delight,
It schemes and dreams in the pale moonlight.
A drape of comfort, a playful tease,
This woolly yarn brings joy with ease.

So here's to that cozy embrace,
A chuckling friend in a frantic race.
With every wear, it tells a grin,
A stitched-up tale that never wears thin.

Fleeting Touches

Once it danced on a wrinkled chair,
Whispering secrets, causing quite a scare.
It met a nose, gave a tickling sneeze,
And rolled off the table with the greatest of ease.

Flicked by a cat, it flew through the air,
A grand adventure, without a care.
It tangled with spoons in the kitchen drawer,
A fashion statement, but who could ignore?

The Warmth of Yesterday

Cozy and bright in the winter chill,
Perfectly wrapped, it gave quite a thrill.
But after a spill of that hot cocoa,
It thought, 'Is this fashion?' Oh no, no, no!

Forgotten in puffs of the laundry's embrace,
Tangled with socks in a textile race.
A hopeful reminder of days that were fine,
Now a relic that's lost track of time.

Echoing Comfort

In the corner, it sat, all fluff and fluff,
Keeping old memories, yet feeling quite tough.
It once warmed a neck on a snowy day,
Now it contemplates life in a drab old way.

A dog found delight in its colorful fold,
Played tug-of-war, so brave and so bold.
But lo and behold, the fun did not cease,
As it became the champion of fashion's decrease.

The Color of a Forgotten Journey

A rainbow spun bright, but colors will fade,
Chasing old dreams in the sun and the shade.
It traveled through times worn chasing delight,
From bustling bazaars to the stillness of night.

It slipped on a bench shared with a friend,
Whispered sweet gossip, oh where would it end?
But perched on a hook, it now plays the fool,
Life's grand escapade, left forgotten at school.

The Enfolded Past

In a drawer deep, a tale unspools,
Colors forgotten, like silly fools.
Twists of fabric chime and cheer,
Laughing at moments now far and near.

A tangled mess, yet it still sways,
Whispering secrets of long-lost days.
Each loop a giggle, each thread a jest,
In the pile of fluff, oh yes, I jest!

Beneath the dust, it dreams away,
Of wacky times, in its own way.
Each loop a chuckle, a stitch so bright,
How did it get here, a funny sight!

Remembering fashion faux pas so grand,
Worn with pride, yet hard to stand.
In every fold, a quirky laugh,
Yarns of humor in this woven craft.

Refinement in Relaxation

Casual days call for clumsy wraps,
Where elegance fades and laughter snaps.
A pile of snug, with quirks galore,
Who said couture can't be a bore?

Fluffy layers, just draped right,
Making fashion a comical plight.
The well-dressed days seem far away,
In playful knots, we find our sway.

With sleeves that fumble and curls that tease,
I strut my stuff with relative ease.
Oh, how they stare, surprised and wide,
At this 'fashion' gig that's gone for a ride!

In this mess, I find my grace,
A comfy hug, my favorite space.
Refinement giggles at my front door,
As I trip and laugh, demanding more!

Yarn of Longing

A single thread, caught in a dream,
Whispers of laughter, or so it seems.
Wishing for travels, adventures bold,
Mapping the tales that have yet to unfold.

Knit by knit, I weave my hope,
For humor and joy to help me cope.
Longing for laughter, with every stitch,
Creating a smile, that's my niche!

In a ball of wool, a world I seek,
While draping my worries, feeling unique.
Oh, custodians of quirky yarn,
Guide my heart to where laughs are born!

Every tug brings a giggle or two,
As I shape this tale, both old and new.
In the knots of fate, joy will unfurl,
In the yarn of longing, let's spin and twirl!

Layers of Gentle Love

Every fold bears a chuckle so sweet,
Wrapped with warmth, it's a delightful treat.
In gentle curves, a kindness we find,
Spreading joy, it's humor unconfined.

Tangled twists, like hugs they embrace,
In comic moments, find your place.
With every layer, love has a face,
A laugh here and there, in this fabric space.

Crinkled edges tell tales of the heart,
Of silly dances and living art.
Through the warmth of fibers, stories align,
Layers of laughter in love's design.

So wrap me snug in this playful thread,
In layers soft, where humor has spread.
Gentle loves dance in fibers so bright,
In the quilt of life, all is delight!

The Silent Garment

In a drawer, so snuggly tight,
Lies a fabric with tales of delight.
It whispers of warmth in the cold,
And giggles of stories yet untold.

Oh, the knots it's tied, both silly and grand,
From a toddler's wild, wandering hand.
It danced with a breeze, then fell off a chair,
A cloak for a cat in a dramatic affair.

On laundry day, it's a wrinkled mess,
Speckled with crumbs, oh what a stress!
Yet every fold has a laugh or a cry,
Like memories that flutter, and never say bye.

So here lies the secret, in laughter and fluff,
A piece of our lives, even when tough.
For though it seems silent, don't you despair,
It's bursting with joy, in its colorful wear.

Weaving Dreams

Threads of ambition in shades of blue,
Stitched with a chuckle, and a peekaboo.
Worn on a whim, for an epic night,
It twirls in the corner, ready for flight.

Each fiber a dream, spun with glee,
Chasing a cold breeze, wild and free.
It caught in the bushes, oh what a sight,
Flapping and flailing, quite the delight!

A twist here, a knot there, what a grand show,
Juggling the laughs as it steals the flow.
With stories of parties and echoes of fun,
It wraps 'round the neck, outshining the sun!

So let's raise a toast to this quirky delight,
Taking our lives to dazzling heights.
In every flutter, and every fold,
Are a million adventures, waiting to be told.

Memories Worn Close

With colors that faded yet gleamed on my throat,
It wraps around stories, as dreams float.
A picnic on grass, with crumbs in the weave,
Each tangle a chuckle, hard to believe.

Whispers of laughter on a breezy walk,
It snatched at a branch, oh how it can talk!
Silly debates it heard in the sun,
Where tales grew taller, and all had their fun.

Each twist and each turn, a playful sway,
Caught in a whirlwind, or lost in a fray.
A hug for my neck, through joy and through tears,
This quirky old fabric holds all my years.

So cherish the moments in threadbare attire,
Each stitch is a giggle, each tear is a choir.
The whispers of memory, with laughter they boast,
Are a fragrant bouquet, I cherish the most.

The Tapestry of Solitude

In a corner it sits, in solitude grand,
A masterpiece woven by a whimsical hand.
Threads of bright colors, a riotous blend,
Grinning with secrets that time cannot bend.

It tells of a dinner, that one fateful night,
When spaghetti tangoed, oh what a sight!
The sauce it now harbors, the stains of the feast,
It chuckles at mishaps, from West to the East.

Each tug has a tale, and every pull sways,
Remembering moments that brightened our days.
Tied in a bow, or looped with finesse,
It wraps life's adventures, a fabric caress.

Embrace the absurd, in every single fold,
For it holds a world, both daring and bold.
Hidden in laughter, and moments that bless,
Is the tapestry threading our whimsical mess.

The Cozy Embrace

In a corner sat a bundle so tight,
Crafted of colors, oh what a sight!
It tickled the chin of a jolly old chap,
As he fumbled and flailed in a wooly mishap.

A cat stalked near, with a gleam in her eyes,
Pouncing on warmth, while the scarf waves bye-bye.
With each silly tussle, as fibers entwine,
They danced around laughter, so silly, divine!

Oh, the knots of the past, so numerous and bold,
With stories of warmth and comfort retold.
Each loop tells a tale, of jests and delight,
As they twirl around the room, what a playful sight!

So here's to the threads that tickle and tease,
Bringing a chuckle, a smile, or a sneeze.
In the land of cozy, under playful weather,
They whisper of fun, as they hang together!

Secrets in the Knots

Oh, the knots in the fabric, a secretive crew,
Hiding their stories, known but to few.
Each twist and each turn, a giggle ensues,
When caught in a tangle, they sing the blues!

A rabbit once tried to hop through the loop,
But ended up tangled, a hilarious scoop!
With threads all askew, he twitched and he grinned,
As he pulled on the fibers, delighting in spins.

A squirrel surveyed from a high-up tree,
Watching the chaos with such glee.
With a flick of his tail, he added to the fuss,
An acorn rained down, what a joyful bus!

So rally your friends, let's unfurl this cheer,
Grab hold of the knots that spark joy and jeer.
In the world of the tangled, so goofy and bright,
The secrets unwind amidst laughter and light!

A Tangle of Warmth

In a pile of yarn, where the laughter is spun,
Lies a tangle of warmth, full of giggles and fun.
With mismatched colors, a riotous blend,
It warms up the smiles of anyone, friend!

A dog dashed past, oh what a surprise,
Wrapped in the fibers, he twirled and he flies.
With a bark and a roll, he claimed his domain,
In a fabric so cozy, he swirled like a hurricane!

A toast to the moments so silly and bright,
When laughter emerges, a whimsical sight.
So gather your pals, and join in the spree,
In this tangle of warmth, wild spirits run free!

Every twist has a tale, each loop has a rhyme,
In the joyful embrace, we dance through time.
So let's celebrate all the quirks that we share,
In this cozy conundrum, no worries or care!

Chronicles of the Thread

In the chronicles spun by a crafty old hand,
Lie tales full of mischief, all perfectly planned.
Each fiber holds secrets of silliness dear,
As laughter unravels, our worries disappear.

A playful raccoon once thought he was slick,
Tangled in threads made of colors so quick.
With a struggle and wiggle, he put on a show,
As he painted a portrait of chaos in tow!

Now, the threads bear witness to moments so bright,
Like the cat who got stuck in a loop of pure light.
With a flick of her paw, she turned quite the scene,
While the laughter erupted, like bubbles, it seemed!

So here's to the stories, woven with glee,
In the chronicles of thread, so wild, so free.
May we celebrate joy, in each twist and each turn,
As we gather together, for laughter we yearn!

A Memory's Embrace

In the attic, I found a weave,
Of colors bright, it made me believe.
Laughing at frays, oh what a sight,
This tale of yarn, both silly and tight.

Once wrapped around my neck so small,
It danced in the breeze, then took a fall.
A pigeon once thought it's a nest,
I chased it away, but laughed with zest.

Now draped on the chair, it's fading fast,
Each thread a remembrance, a laugh from the past.
It whispers stories of wormy delight,
Oh, those silly days in the warm sunlight.

So here's to this knit, a tangled delight,
A fabric that giggles, oh what a sight!
In memories, it wraps me with glee,
A humorous hug, forever with me.

Knitted Nostalgia

Woolly and warm, with patterns all wrong,
It tickles my neck, like a silly song.
Each loop and twist, a funny mistake,
But hold it just right, and oh, what a break!

Once the star of a chill evening's glow,
Now joined by dust, it surely won't flow.
The dog claimed it first, like a prize at a fair,
With teeth marks aplenty and threads in the air.

When friends come around for a cozy night,
They chuckle at it, oh what a sight!
This knitted companion, not quite a friend,
But oh, the humor, it will never end!

So here it remains, a nostalgic cheer,
With stories and laughter, it holds ever near.
In the fabric of life, it softly unfurls,
A warm knitted memory, wrapping the world.

Fluttering Comfort

Bright colors swirl like a circus show,
Finding new life in the breeze's flow.
A friendly flutter, a giggle or two,
It dances around, just chasing its cue.

Once tangled in bushes, a squirrel found fame,
It chewed on a corner to make it a game.
Oh, how we laughed as it flapped and spun,
A scarf with a story, always full of fun!

In the rain, I wore it, a makeshift hat,
Squished like a pancake, oh what of that!
Yet comfort it brought, with each droplet's kiss,
A soggy reminder, I wouldn't dismiss.

So here is the tale of this fluttering friend,
It brings joy and laughter that never will end.
A whimsical element, forever in tow,
A fabric delight, with its playful show.

Tides of Fabric

Oh, the tides of fabric, waving so free,
A playful journey, just like the sea.
With curls and swirls, it's caught in the sun,
Each ripple a giggle, oh what fun!

Once lost in the laundry, it took a wild dive,
With socks in the wild—the ultimate live!
When I finally found it, it wore a proud grin,
A salty adventure, where had it been?

Now wrapped around my shoulders with style,
It whispers of fun in every big smile.
From beach to the park, it's got tales untold,
With every twist, it gets bolder and bold!

So let me cherish this fabric so fine,
For in all its waves, I can't help but shine.
A tapestry woven with laughter and cheer,
The tides of fabric, forever held dear.

Knots of Love

In a drawer, tucked away,
A twisted yarn begins to sway.
It giggles at the knots it makes,
Tying heartstrings, just for laughs.

Colors clash, a vibrant show,
Hitching rides on breezy flow.
Each loop a tale of silly bites,
Where frizzy ends become delights.

Whispering secrets in a twist,
A tangled dance, too good to miss.
It wraps around a friend so dear,
Who shares a laugh and brings good cheer.

So let the threads entwine and spin,
For every knot's a chuckle within.
A playful journey, soft and bold,
In threads of humor, joys unfold.

Loops of Time

In circles round, a funny twist,
Each loop finds joy, how could it resist?
A tangled past, a comet's flight,
Time dances on, both wrong and right.

Knots of moments, woven tight,
The laughter echoes through the night.
With every pull and snug embrace,
Time trips along, a playful chase.

A brother's prank, a sister's tease,
With every loop, giggles tease.
Time loops around to share a smile,
In each soft weave, a love worthwhile.

So mess it up, don't make it neat,
For life's a loop that can't be beat.
Let the threads tell their tale in rhyme,
For laughter weaves through loops of time.

Laying Under the Weaving Sky

Beneath the hues of sunset glow,
A fabric world begins to flow.
Threads of laughter float on high,
As we lay under the weaving sky.

Clouds play games of hide and seek,
Rolling softly, playful and meek.
We chuckle as the breezes tease,
Beneath the threads of rustling leaves.

Unraveled dreams drift in the breeze,
Whispering jokes that put us at ease.
As kites that dance in reckless flight,
Woven tales take off in delight.

So laugh aloud, let spirits fly,
In every fiber, a sweet goodbye.
A patchwork quilt of joy on high,
While lying under the weaving sky.

Echoes in Woven Threads

In the fabric, echoes sing,
Woven tales that laughter bring.
With quirky knots and silly bends,
Each stitch a tale of funny friends.

A grandma's yarn, a grandpa's joke,
In every thread, a giggle woke.
Silly patterns and vibrant hues,
Dancing as the mystery brews.

A curious cat joins in the play,
Pouncing on threads that roam away.
The laughter rolls, a joyful blend,
In echoes that the fabric sends.

So weave a tale, release the giggles,
Where laughter hides and sweet time wiggles.
With every knot and twist so free,
Echoes of joy in threads we see.

A Symphony of Silken Stories

In a spool, a symphony sways,
Silken stories sing through days.
Each thread a note with whimsy traced,
Woven tunes that can't be replaced.

A fuss and fumble, a dance in time,
Silly tales blend in sweet rhyme.
Knots of laughter and gentle sighs,
Each stitch a waltz under blue skies.

Chasing dreams with every swirl,
A tapestry where giggles unfurl.
The fabric giggles in harmony,
A melody of yarn so free.

So let the tales continue to play,
In silken whispers, come what may.
For in the weaves of laughter's lore,
We find the joy we can't ignore.

Cloaked in Seasons Past

In autumn's chill, it hugs my neck,
A witness to the time I'd wreck.
Each thread a story, each stitch a laugh,
Dancing with joy in a warm photograph.

Winter's snowflakes, a twinkling dance,
My trusty wrap—a fashion chance!
In spring, it flutters like a butterfly,
Twirling around, oh how time flies!

Summer's heat? It hangs on tight,
Laughing at sweats, a silly sight.
With colors bright, it jests away,
In wardrobe wars, it's here to stay.

The Comfort of Fabric Dreams

In dreams of fabric, I take a ride,
Tangles of yarn, oh what a slide!
Frolicking threads in whimsical shoes,
Chasing laughter and cozy hues.

Patterns clash like socks on a date,
Hilarity swirls; we laugh, we relate.
A pillow fort made from moth-eaten wool,
Napping away, in playful drool.

With each little pull, it whispers cheer,
Stories of comfort, stitched sincere.
So here's a tale of fluff and glee,
In threads of laughter, we roam free.

Soft Shadows in a Chaotic World

In a whirlwind of colors, I whirl about,
Loop-de-loops, oh what's that about?
A tangled mess, but oh! What a show,
Soft shadows dancing like a fluffy glow.

In chaos, it chuckles, what a delight,
As I trip on the hem, oh what a sight!
The fabric giggles, plays hide and seek,
Whispering secrets, a world unique.

Through the clutter, its silliness beams,
Stitching together our wildest dreams.
With grace it tumbles, oh what a twirl,
In chaos, it shines, causing a whirl.

Love Knitted in Everyday Life

Two needles clicking, a rhythm divine,
Knitting smiles with fibers entwined.
Every purl a hug, each knit a kiss,
In cozy moments, we find our bliss.

A warm embrace on a chilly day,
Interwoven giggles, come what may.
In every loop, a memory stored,
Love stitched tight, in colors adored.

Through the clatter and bustle, we find our way,
Woven together, come laugh what may.
In the fabric of life, the threads are pure,
For love is found in stitches we endure.

A Woven Story

In tangled threads, a laugh does hide,
Each twist and turn, a silly ride.
A cat once claimed it as his bed,
In dreams of yarn, he bumped his head.

Colors clash in a playful dance,
Patterns swirl like a child's prance.
Dropped in soup, a noodle's fate,
"Too cozy!" muttered a confused plate.

From Grandma's stash, it spans the years,
Collecting dust, but no regrets or fears.
Worn on days of sunshine bright,
Or nights that call for warmth, not fright.

So when you see it draped with glee,
Remember the tales, wild and free.
In every fold, a memory peeks,
A woven story that softly speaks.

The Softness of Time

A cozy hug in the winter's chill,
It wraps around you, a gentle thrill.
Gone are the days of looking frumpy,
In this fluffy cloud, we feel quite jumpy.

Worn on a ride upon a bike,
Its threads are tales of a friendly hike.
At times it acts like a flying cap,
Of silly images, it's a perfect map.

Stains of cocoa, and crumbs of cake,
In its fibers, memories awake.
With every thread, a chuckle flows,
In the softness, the joy overflows.

So here's to the wraps that tell a joke,
To all the warmth in every cloak.
Time softens edges, both sharp and loud,
In laughter's embrace, we're ever proud.

Loops of Lost Moments

Circles of fabric, a loop so wide,
Tangled with laughter, they never hide.
Moments loop back, fun times we've shared,
With each little tuck, we're meta-prepared.

Once dropped at a party, it took a dive,
Pet goldfish thought it was quite alive!
Neighbors would joke, "Where's that thing been?"
It's just collecting stories from the unseen.

The sun fades, and so does that stain,
But the giggles linger, like a playful chain.
From a child's tantrum to a grandmas' cheer,
These loops hold more than just fashion here.

With colors bright and patterns bold,
It keeps the silly and stories untold.
Wrapped up tightly in life's grand jest,
In the laughs we share, we find our best.

Beneath the Wrapping

Under this layer of fuzzy grace,
Silly moments find their place.
A peacock strutting, all decked in flair,
A surprise awaits with every wear.

Twirling round in a kitchen so bright,
This playful wrap turns day to night.
In the warmth of blankets, we giggle and chat,
"Did it just whisper?" "Oh, imagine that!"

Puppies chase threads, dancing on toes,
As playful yarn in the corner grows.
A treasure map, if only you knew,
Of the giggles hidden inside, just for you.

Wrapped around secrets, snug and tight,
Each fiber whispers, "What's next tonight?"
So here's to moments that never lack,
Beneath this wrapping, joy's always back.

The Fabric of Memories

In a drawer, I once found a thread,
That tied my socks, but they fled.
They danced and pranced in playful cheer,
A sock ballet, oh dear, oh dear!

A button rolled right off the shelf,
Claiming it simply lost itself.
So many tales woven tight,
Each stitch, a giggle in the night.

The quilt whispers secrets so bold,
Of tea spills and tales long told.
Every patch has a wink and a smile,
Stitching joy, oh, all the while.

Oh, the fabric of laughter, a patchwork divine,
A sofa fort made from cloth and twine.
Memories tucked in each crooked seam,
A tapestry of giggles, forever a dream.

Echoes Beneath the Stitch

Once I stitched a bear with a head,
But forgot its arms, oh what dread!
It waved with its ears, such a sight,
That quirky grin gave me a fright!

Through seams and hems, I found the fun,
A quirky patch for everyone.
Each little thread, a joke unwound,
With every knot, pure laughter found.

A needle pricked such silly glee,
As fabric tales danced wild and free.
Echoes of laughter in each fold,
Adventures in fabric, daring and bold.

What's that in the pocket? A cat?
With yarn left trailing, imagine that!
In every stitch, a world anew,
Echoes of chaos in cloth, it's true!

Embrace of the Twisted Yarn

In the basket, yarn is a whirl,
Knitted chaos, a twist and a twirl.
A tangled mess makes the cutest hats,
Hilarious styles, oh how it chats!

I tried to crochet a simple square,
But ended up with a monster, I swear!
It blinked and sighed, with googly eyes,
Saying, 'Wear me, please!'—what a surprise!

One spool sings with a voice so bright,
It hums and buzzes throughout the night.
A playful dance with each little loop,
Creating mischief, a woolly troop!

In the embrace of yarn, joy resides,
With goofy patterns and snuggly rides.
Each twist and turn, a giggle parade,
In this wild world, let laughter invade!

Hues of Remembrance

Once I colored a canvas so bold,
With every hue, a memory told.
But slipped in the purple, oh what a plight,
It turned my cat into a funny sight!

A paintbrush dabbed on grandma's chair,
Now it looks like a monster from the lair.
Yet every splash brings a grin so wide,
Recalling moments with joy and pride.

In swirls of color, laughter does blend,
As stories emerge around each bend.
What color's next? A rainbow dance,
In vivid echoes, a playful romance.

Hues of remembrance, forever bright,
With every brushstroke, pure delight.
In the palette of life, hues entwine,
We craft our stories, quirky and fine!

A Dance of Fabric and Frost

In the closet, hidden tight,
A dance of fabric takes its flight.
With every twist and little spin,
It giggles softly, lets joy in.

Once worn by a dog named Lou,
It flopped and flailed, what a view!
With pompoms bouncing, colors flash,
While Dust Bunnies cheer, 'Oh what a crash!'

Caught in the breeze, oh what a sight,
It twirls and twines, pure delight.
Friends with buttons, glee untold,
Together they weave stories bold.

A saga spun with threads so spry,
Frolicking 'neath the winter sky.
Oh, in this world of weave and knit,
Who knew such fun could ever fit?

When Threads Meet Time

Two threads collide, a dizzy dance,
In the drawer, they take a chance.
One's from winter, snug and warm,
The other's flair, a summertime charm.

They bicker softly, pinching tight,
'You're too bold!' 'You're just polite!'
In this patchwork of goofy dreams,
They weave mishaps, or so it seems.

Once a belt, a bow, a hat,
Now a cape for a playful cat.
Fleeting moments tickle the air,
As they laugh off all their wear and tear.

A tale of threads now stitched with glee,
Against the clock, they frolic free.
With each giggle, they boldly climb,
Together they conquer the sands of time.

The Gentle Hand of Memory

A gentle pull from the old trunk,
Whispers stories, fragrant funk.
Softly it shares with every fold,
Memories wrapped in colors bold.

Once a toddler's cherished wish,
Now a quirky, festive dish.
It sways as if to say, 'Remember?'
The joy of cold nights, bright December.

It's knitted knots of laughter bright,
Flashing back to playful nights.
With fuzzy stories, it does declare,
Time's just a thread in the fabric fair.

So here you are, stitched with grace,
Each pattern holds a smiling face.
With every loop and every seam,
Old memories laugh, like a happy dream.

Wrapped in Timelessness

Under the stars, it wraps so tight,
A cloak of warmth in the moonlight.
It snickers softly, a playful tease,
'Wanna know my tales, if you please?'

Once an heirloom, once a draft,
Now a costume in a child's craft.
Unraveled joy, a colorful spree,
Each swirl a hug, oh do you see?

With every twist, it swishes round,
Tickling toes, then on the ground.
It questions all, 'What do you wear?'
And giggles softly, without a care.

Time stands still when the fabric spins,
In laughter's game, who really wins?
With every wrap, a secret dance,
Wrapped in joy, life's funny chance.

www.ingramcontent.com/pod-product-compliance
Lightning Source LLC
Chambersburg PA
CBHW050308120526
44590CB00016B/2543